# THEORY OF TWILIGHT
## by
### Gary Short

*For Dick & Mardath*

*This book comes to you in the name of shared empathy toward nature, life, landscape.*

*My Best,*
*Gary*
*12/19/95*
*American Flat, Nevada*

## Ahsahta Press
### Boise State University
### Boise, Idaho

# Acknowledgments

***Brushfire***: "Near Mina"
***The Chariton Review***: "George Pascho Miller"; "The Mare Slept Standing"; "Ornament"; "Yes"
***Cimarron Review:*** "Grace"
***Hayden's Ferry Review:*** "A White Rock"
***Midwest Quarterly:*** "Toward Morning"; "Trajectory"
***Napa Review:*** "Test"
***Painted Hills Review:*** "Salt"; "Third Grade: Later in November, 1963"
***Passages North:*** "Lines on an Autumn Night"
***Permafrost:*** "Brothers Playing Catch on Christmas Day"; "Dancing with the One-Armed Girl"; "Silver"; "Unionville Spring"
***Poetry East:*** "The Design of Pain"; "Sophal Niem and the Moon in the Bucket"; part three of "The Waiting," titled "After My Brother's Death"
***Poetry Now:*** "On a Windy Afternoon"; "Two Poems About Wells, Nevada"
***Quarterly West:*** "Bare Trees"; "Boundaries"; "Evidence"
***Shankpainter:*** "Theory of Twilight"
***Writers' Forum:*** "Arizona"; "Field of Vision"; "Photograph"; "Rains"
***Handspan of Red Earth: An Anthology of American Farm Poems*** (edited by Catherine Lewallen Marconi, University of Iowa Press, 1991): "Ornament"
***Desert Wood*** (edited by Shaun Griffin, University of Nevada Press, 1991): "Near Mina"; "Test"; "Toward Morning"; "Two Poems About Wells, Nevada"
***Seven Nevada Poets*** (edited by William L. Fox, Rainshadow Editions, 1991): "Driving Highway 93: Nevada"

"Sophal Niem and the Moon in the Bucket" will appear in an anthology of writers from the Fine Arts Work Center to be published by Sheep Meadow Press.

"Brothers Playing Catch on Christmas Day" was printed as a broadside by Karla Elling for Mummy Mountain Press, Arizona State University.

Some of these poems appeared in the chapbook, ***Looking Past Today*** (Duck Down Press)

I am thankful to the Fine Arts Work Center in Provincetown, the Nevada State Council on the Arts, and the Ludwig Vogelstein Foundation for their support; also to Centrum, the MacDowell Colony and the Tuscarora School of Pottery for residencies.

Big thanks for Charlie Buck. And to Norman Dubie, Dennis Schmitz, Scott Shaddock, Janet Sylvester, and Judith Vollmer, my gratitude.

Editor for Ahsahta Press: Tom Trusky

***Theory of Twilight***
is printed on acid-free text and cover papers.

Copyright ©1994 by Gary Short

ISBN 0-916272-58-3

Library of Congress Catalog Card Number:
93-72425

*For Catherine French*

*And in memory
of
Richard Short 1941-1980
George Miller 1959-1986*

# Contents

Introduction *by Norman Dubie* ................................................................iii

## One

Driving Highway 93: Nevada ...............................................................3
Letter from Alva Greer to his Sister, Joanna: 1867, Virginia City ..........4
A White Rock................................................................................5
Third Grade: Later in November, 1963 ...............................................6
Evidence ......................................................................................7
Two Poems About Wells, Nevada.......................................................8
Arizona........................................................................................9
Brothers Playing Catch on Christmas Day.........................................10
Grace ........................................................................................11
Photograph.................................................................................12
Field of Vision ............................................................................13
George Pascho Miller ...................................................................14

## Two

The Mare Slept Standing...............................................................19
The Design of Pain ......................................................................20
Ornament ..................................................................................22
Lines on an Autumn Night.............................................................23
Near Mina..................................................................................24
Dancing with the One-Armed Girl ..................................................25
Bare Trees .................................................................................26
Toward Morning..........................................................................27
Unionville Spring ........................................................................28
Rains ........................................................................................29
Theory of Twilight .......................................................................30

## Three

Yes............................................................................................35
Sophal Niem and the Moon in the Bucket........................................36
Salt ..........................................................................................38

i

Silver ..................................................................................................40
Trajectory .........................................................................................42
Test ...................................................................................................43
Boundaries .......................................................................................44
On a Windy Afternoon ...................................................................46
The Waiting .....................................................................................47

NOTE: A centered asterisk indicates a poem has been broken mid-stanza.

# Introduction

The wildly androgynous Bengali saint, Ramakrishna Paramahamsa, sat beneath the white gulchi trees of his Dakshineswar temple in our terrible time of the Kali Yuga and pronounced this modest story to his young disciples:

There was a firebird that lived so high in the ether that surrounds our planet that she is never permitted by her aspirations to touch the land. One late afternoon out of boredom the sun visited the firebird, impregnating her. Shortly afterward she produced a large buff egg which immediately began to plummet toward the earth. But because the firebird's element was so removed from us, and because the egg heated as it fell through our atmosphere, a young firebird hatched from the shell still miles from the ground. The young firebird tumbled in wonder for some while and then suddenly fledged, gained its wings and executed a perfect arc upward avoiding by seconds the snowy crags of one of the earth's tallest mountains.

This is my best recollection of what is obviously a story about spirituality but it is also a legend we might tell ourselves about inspiration in poetry. Didn't Rilke suggest that if you fell far enough you'd probably arrive in the land of the arisen? I believe the full courage of this aesthetic and its regard for experience is everywhere in Gary Short's remarkable first book of poems, **Theory of Twilight**. Take for example this passage from the title poem in the volume. This is an elegy for the poet's brother:

> I took the card down and walked out
>     into the hallway's sallow light. My parents
> were coming toward me. Mother rushed the room,
>     but we held her back. I'm not sure why.
> She called out his name and her voice drifted
>
>     back thirty years—a mother's evening song,
> lilting across the deep-rutted road into the summer field,
>     calling him home.
> While my father entered the room, I held the pain-
>     keeping grief
>
> against her small shoulder until the door opened
>     and he took her in.
> A stunning sunset in Mollendo, and I

>     was missing everyone I'd ever loved.
> The door opened on the last glimpse of my brother.
>
>         He was not as I had left him.
> His father had touched his eyes closed, mothered
>         the shock of black hair from his forehead
> and made into prayer, finger by finger
>         the hands.

In this poem of death and transfiguration the dead brother's physical hands are nearly muted alchemically into prayer or grace. In many of Short's harshest poems of childhood and life in Nevada there is always this plunging vertical emotion that exhausts both its momentum and its rhetoric and then some magical translation occurs that is against all theories of twilight and all experiences of any life that takes its phrasing from a sense of tragic barriers. So what I'm saying is that this is a heroic poetry but dedicated to ordinary lives in which, as the title of this poem indicates, "the mare must sleep standing":

> On her way to the bus-stop, the neighbor girl
> carries North America in her hands
> a large map veined with river,
> blue threads glued to cardboard.
> When the mare was born glazed and still,
> the girl's father punched its chest, forced
> his own breath into the mouth and nostrils
> until the foal returned to life.
>
> My breath makes a moon on the window.
> The horse marks new snow with hoofprints
> homing toward shelter.
> From the woodpile I'll bring pieces of pine
> dusted with snow. The wood will give
> warmth I need, the flame exactly blue.

There is something William Carlos Williams would think to praise in this book's saddest poems where the lost, the fallen, the young, and the vulnerable are all finding themselves shaped into hopeless ciphers finding hope. What we must mark about this work besides its grace and courage, its reckless sentiment becoming song, is its final refusal of solitude—that very solitude that accumulates poems, that paginates books and says to you, reader: **Now we are two!** This book without the great wind of a Whitman or an Emerson is about union. That is the American theme and these poems are the falling birth of a very gifted and young American poet.

*Norman Dubie*
Tempe, Arizona
July, 1993

We learn as the thread plays out, that we belong
less to what flatters us than to what scars.

*—Stanley Kunitz*

# One

# Driving Highway 93: Nevada

Ritual of the wheel in my hands,
the highway's long trance at the center of night,
nothing but these miles
& no swerving until

headlights,
four bright lights—
a car passing another,
headlights brighter, larger
& no place for me to go—
I jerk hard right & floor it
into the desert.

                Mist of dust drifting white.
When the jarring stops,
the shudder & stall of the car
is my heart. In two streams of ghost light
the red eyes of bored open-range cattle,
dust settling calm on their backs.
The cars I swerved to avoid
become taillights,
red eyes closing into night,

& the moon
through black broken clouds
is a mask

or a premonition

the way dust smells like rain
before it rains.

# Letter from Alva Greer to His Sister, Joanna: 1867, Virginia City

This will be quickly told. You said you might come west if I wrote with recommendation. I wish you would not. One pair of sad eyes, those of my darling wife Edith, is ample weight for me to haul. I miss you. But I fear this land is not for one of your stripe. There is much space and it is filled with loneliness.

We have lost our dear one. Rachel preferred another place. She died January 9. I recall her playing the part of an angel. Holding her hands piously together and flying about the room. From our savings I had made a stone angel with the face of a child to mark her grave.

There is snow and chill underfoot. Edith reads the English poet Browning by lamplight. I cannot love her enough. I will go to teaching or take a position as secretary for one of the companies. My investments in the mines are as fallow as my fields in Iowa. I have made mistakes but I am not a bad man.

Today I visited the cemetery. It is outside of town on a hill barren of ore. But I have something more precious in the ground than silver. Snow was feathering down upon the white angel.

I do not think I will soon find the path homeward, I wish I could take wings and sail. I should like you to send a likeness for me to place on the wall. Attend to your schooling. May God grant you good things. This is my prayer. I am your brother, Alva

# A White Rock

I wondered about the moon
& at the river a dead rabbit
was spinning in an eddy, a strange furred fish
with the curved back of a migrant. I saw
my grandfather cuss his own body,
throw his paralyzed arm against the wall,
"You no good sonofafuck."

I recall the thin hand on the face of his old watch
lurching forward second by second.
Each day from school I kicked a different rock—
& stones gathered near the driveway—
so many homecomings.
I thought about the husband of the woman next door.
He went away & never came back.

Later, on a night when the moon
tired even Orion,
I said three words
to a girl in an asparagus field,
& she pressed a white rock into my hand,
closed my fingers tight around it. I wanted
to bury the full unbalance of desire
in the furrowed earth irrigated with moonlight.

# Third Grade: Later in November, 1963

Tracing letters on granular paper
between wide blue margins, I gripped too hard
the thick pencil, my middle finger
blistering. On the wall
posters pictured the sacred journey of milk
from cow to carton.

                      That Friday,
only Adrian Vucinich cried when our teacher cried.
Mrs. Gray held a white handkerchief, led us
through, "America the Beautiful."
The falsetto of nine-year-old boys vibrated
water in the fishbowl where guppies,
enlarged by refraction, stared big-eyed
around the room at thirty-one paper turkeys
with thumb heads & fingered fantails.

A photograph of the President's wife
crawling onto the trunk of a black convertible;
my father, silent, went outside to rake
piles of magnolia leaves;
on television, a handcuffed man
crumpled slow-motion to the floor again...

The blowing half-mast flag snapped in the wind.
At recess Clayton Shedd shouted
a dog had been hit by a car.
Our class ran to the chain-link fence to look,
pressing against the geometry of the metal,
& there within the crosswalk borders
in front of the school the dog lay dying.
When I pulled away from what I saw, turned
to go back to third grade,
the fence had left its gauge on my hands.

# Evidence

The bloody florets in the dust
by the roadside are paw prints
of my cat three days gone—

the scratch at the door, small yowl
in the wind.

Where am I to look for him?
Here is the grim evidence.
I echo & re-echo the old grade school rule—
a preposition is anywhere a cat can go.

I think of the hurt cat limping away
through the brush, fiddleneck & gold-back fern,
around the drainage ditch & across
the twisted orchard.

These blood blossoms
are not proof. As long as I don't find the cat,
I keep it alive,

my life haunted
by what I already know
but don't want to.

# Two Poems About Wells, Nevada

1)    A Poem Overheard in K.G.'s Bar

      This is the only town I know
      where you can stand up to your ass in snow

      & still
      have dust blow in your eye




2)    A Poem Blown Away By the Wind

# Arizona

When the sparrow flies into the window
it sounds like a worn hammerhead on piano wire.
Then the bird lies a lost note
on the pale-green patio.

The child who goes outside to find it
already knows broken things.
The neck limp, a bead eye, wary, blinks.
The still-living bird, a small fist
curled in sleep, is taken inside the house
it tried to fly through
and placed in a shoebox where rocks, pinecones,
and a blue feather had been kept.

Where did it come from? the child asks,
and mother takes the bird book from the shelf.
On page 312 they find sage sparrow—
white spot below the ear, a single brown mark
on the clear breast. A song of four to seven notes,
the third note highest.

The mother says the bird has come from winter
in Arizona, and tomorrow they will see if it can fly.
Shoebox by the bed, the child lies awake
wondering what else will break against glass
and thinks of Arizona as the place where pain comes from—
small shadow over the earth
to a backyard in Reno.

# Brothers Playing Catch on Christmas Day

Only a little light remains.
The new football feels heavy
and our throws are awkward,
like the conversation of brothers
who see each other occasionally.
After a few exchanges,
confidence grows,
the passing and catching
feels natural and good.
Gradually, we move farther apart,
out in the street,
the space between us
filling with darkness.

He leads me,
lofting perfect spirals
into the night. My eyes
find the clean white laces of the ball.
I let fly a deep pass
to his silhouette.
The return throw
cannot be seen,
yet the ball
falls into my hands, as if
we have established a code
that only brothers know.

# Grace

When she said she was going to fish,
I heard *wish* & followed
down the path to the creek.
It's bluebird weather, grandmother said.
Her fishing pole wavered in the heat,
thin shadow of a limb.

She pulled six catfish from the stream bottom
where they clouded across rock.
I carried them home in a bucket,
the water swirled with twitching & silt.

In the kitchen, grandmother
held a catfish in her garden glove,
warning me about the barbs & spined fins
as she placed the fish on a warped board
laid across the sink,
took a nail & hammered
head to wood.

The nail skidded on mud-green skin,
viscous & unyielding, the fish
flipped from the board & slapped on the floor,
feelers groping linoleum, tail flapping,
catfish body curved against air.

Grandmother wiped the blood on her apron,
the patterned strawberries smeared red.
She drove the nail home finally
then took pliers, pulled the skin back
by inches until the fish was peeled,

revealed & made strange
like a translucent stone
or my mother's pale hand
asleep on the sheet.
I heard the hammer blows & slipped away
to the wishing creek, tried to hear
the silence between.

# Photograph

We didn't know, but now
we can see a balance has tipped
against him. And now that we see it,
there will never be a time
when we will not see it. His face
an ill-fitting mask
rising away from bone. As a result
his dark brown eyes become a voice,
a moment of recognition . . .

> *It's come to this. I have
> a new language. In four months
> the doctors will open the book
> of my body, read its last pages.*

In this photograph, the clock
is a remark on the wall.
Outside, the sky falls like seconds,
the rain a consecration. My brother's face
will blur as he turns toward the window
to look beyond the bare maple, beyond
what he knows, what I do not know.

# Field of Vision

When I crawled up inside the attic
where knowledge is antecedent
to memory, I could hear—
*We're waltzing in the wonder
of why we're here*, my mother singing
as she ironed my father's shirts.
Earlier I had watched her
spread one arm of his shirt,
then the other, & fold the arms
across the heart.

                I balanced
on dusty beams & inched closer,
brushing past a crate of women's worn shoes
& a box that held pictures
of the girl who would be my mother,
until I perched above her song, afraid
of falling through.
A bare bulb shaped yellow light
all angle from the gable.

                A pair of glasses
in a cigar box, the loop of wire-rims
too big over my ears, & then unfocused color—
the pile of shoes blurred together.
My eyes ached until I took the glasses off,
worked my way back toward the opening
above the hallway.

                Still inside
I closed the trapdoor & pulled the beaded chain
shut into black. Huddled there
in a hollow, I could not tell
where one body ended & the deep water
that joined me to my mother began.

# George Pascho Miller

The windows opened to seven sheep
in my pasture yard, and black Bucephalus
who stood horse-sure, quiet,
in his I-will-be-here-forever stance.
     Driving here
east from Tonopah I could have been a headline
in the **Lincoln County Record**; I barely dodged
three midnight cattle on the open range.
All April I taught in the rural county schools,
staying in this two-room house without television
    or telephone.
Time slowed the way I like it.
I had just written the line, *loving you*
*would have been the dark remembering sun,*
when I heard Williamson's truck
scrape the gravel driveway. He came to the door
and slow drawled, "Your father
just got hold of me. I'm sorry. It's bad news.
A friend of yours was killed last night."
                              I stepped out
into the changed world; the black coat of the horse
    glinted and held sunlight
as if there were no way not to be in this world.
The afternoon calm gained a second wind. The sky,
a clean Nevada blue, obscured nothing
except the name of the lost.
     My father, in his kindness, hadn't said—
wanting me to hear it from him.
In the ten minutes it took to get to Williamson's place,
dust trailing behind us, I wondered what happened
in the sudden night—a car wreck?
or, this being America, a bullet?
                        A vesper sparrow
flickered across the hood
then rose and disappeared in a grace note.
At the place where the bird was subtracted from air

\*

was a list of the names of friends alive,
                              and next to it
a list of the dead. I read the two columns,
then realized I will lose everyone
through death, theirs or mine.
                              I told Williamson
I was tired of bouncing from town to town, I wanted
to find a home, hang on to what I love.
Then I made a crow lift up and fly
from the dead rabbit in the road. In a daydream
I took with my hand a fingerling trout
trapped in a pocket of evaporating water
and released it swimming into the river.
                              Which one was lost to me?
I steadied myself and dialed, the receiver hard
     against my ear
where a name would be.

# Two

# The Mare Slept Standing

When she uncloses her black eyelids
it is winter, the ground white as a Sunday shirt.
The fallen leaves, remaining light
against the body of a weathered Chevy truck.
Two crows lift, a silence rising with them,
they glide over the windbreak of cottonwoods
into another color.
                    When someone dies,
that person is everywhere & nowhere.
Last night under a lean moon I crossed the pasture
& heard the coyote's weirding cry.

On her way to the bus-stop, the neighbor girl
carries North America in her hands
a large map veined with river,
blue threads glued to cardboard.
When the mare was born glazed and still,
the girl's father punched its chest, forced
his own breath into the mouth & nostrils
until the foal returned to life.

My breath makes a moon on the window.
The mare marks new snow with hoofprints
homing toward shelter.
From the woodpile I'll bring pieces of pine
dusted with snow. The wood will give
warmth I need, the flame exactly blue.

# The Design of Pain

I don't know much more now than I did
as a boy that summer

when I would ride my bicycle
down the road to your house,
past fields where fat crows
settled in rows of cut alfalfa.

Although I can't recall your face,
I hear your voice, your laugh
when I told you I was 8 & 3/4.

My parents talked about you over dinner:
city-girl, teacher, divorce, time-away.
I listened, lifted my milk & drank.

You had a dollhouse
with a grandaddy-longlegs
in the small kitchen
you wanted left alone.

We drew dragons in chalk
on your cracked wooden porch,
holding up pink, blue & yellow fingers,

but the pastel washed off too quickly.
One accidental step lifting away
our fragile stay against nothing.

Most of the people I have lied to
I have loved. What am I
to make of that?

Now when I am waiting
for grief to ease
or have hurt someone,
I think of the chalk, your peeling porch
& you.

You fixed a room in the dollhouse
for a boy. A red book on the table,
a ceramic cat on the foot of the bed.
In the corner, a miniature baseball bat.

It was that boy, the dollhouse boy,
who came to visit one day
& stood on a dragon's yellow tail
at the screendoor & heard
you crying, the rattled heaving
a body can make

knowing itself alive & caught
in something too big to order
or hold in the palm like a tiny chiffonnier.

The boy fled, jumped on his red Western Flyer
& pedaled as fast as he could, away
from what he had heard

& toward it.

# Ornament

*for Wally Cuchine*

The children chased tumbleweeds,
blue variations over December snow.
Against the bunkhouse buckaroos watched,
drinking coffee splashed with Jack Daniels.
Steam drifted whiskey on the wind
as the rancher's kids hung silver bells on the thistles
filigreed with ice.

In summer the tin roof on a shack in Unionville
ripples like the snow peak three ranges east.
On the desert the calves are dragged & branded,
singed hide pungent as tarweed burning.
Ray & Dallas look for stragglers along the railway bed
leading to the old silver town.
Their horses' hooves uncover oyster shells
tossed from dining cars a century ago.
The hot air blows a ghost rattle through vetch pods.
Then out of dust whirling counter-sunwise, a tumbleweed
& the broken clink of silver ornament,
illusive & desirable, turns
through sage across the white flats.

# Lines on an Autumn Night

I name the moon mine,
and no one is here
to argue. I listen to the cricket's trill,
the moon in full bloom, my mind

noisy with the worst goodbyes.
Outside the window of leaves, the wind
flirts with the elm. No one
can tell you how to live alone.

No one can tell you
where to find the lost things—
pens, wallets, promise rings.
It's noisy all the time. The moon is mine.

# Near Mina

*for Roger Smith*

For now
this is all there is—
sky, sand & sun.

We travel on a road
unfolding its reverie
through small towns.

Thirty miles from
a quiet place,
a rundown bar,

a sign
with a faded letter C
advertising   OLD BEER.

On the outskirts of town,
a crop
of abandoned cars.

In the distance clouds
lower long ladders
of rain.

Soon damp earth
& sage
will perfume the air.

200 miles
to Las Vegas,
& the hours

huddle together
like cattle seeking solace
from the rain.

# Dancing with the One-Armed Girl

Some of the Senior boys have yet to decide
between Southeast Asia, Canada or prison. The gym

is decorated with green & yellow crepe paper
& a chipped wooden moon that needs paint.

When she asks me to dance I'm afraid of friends' laughter,
but she is more sure than schoolboys are cruel.

I feel the pulse of the arm never found,
never lost,

severed when the speedboat ran over her
& reaching now from the bottom silt of Lake Tahoe.

If I can sense the phantom touch
then she too can feel it & the moment

after, when the body
began to remember itself. The arm

calling back for its body
or perhaps another to hold

as it drifted deeper blues
through lakewater.

Small fish swimming
between fingers of an outstretched hand

like memory brushing against us,
the way her hair touched my cheek.

The air in the gym was deep with currents,
the back of her dress damp with sweat.

The lost arm remains
holding to memory, knowing

the slow dance of lower depths.

# Bare Trees

I stood in a light snow & looked into the grave.
In the hole was a tangle of tendril-like roots
that had been chopped with an ax.

The broken roots were ice.
Very cold. Very strange.
A nightmare nest of leeches,
slick & transparent, they would try
to wriggle their way into the coffin.

I was ten & thought,
God, what a thing
to have grandfather planted there.

Juxtaposed to my fear, the hush of snow
was funereal. The glide of ritual
the adults calmly joined.
My aunt, her mascara thick as a '60's starlet,
cried quietly as we turned to walk away
out of the cold that pressed close & the wind
mourning among old stones & bare trees.

Sometimes I'd sit with grandmother by the fire.
Stars blurred in the four-paned window
where snow sparked in each frame of sky,
a winter scene sealed in a glass dome
& set on a widow's mantel.

She often fell asleep while reading.
Her face was still water,
the white Bible in her lap
slanting like a tombstone.
The log would snap in the fireplace
& sparks scatter red
a moment. I would think about winter
& what it buries.

# Toward Morning

The sky sleek as the coat of a blue roan
in the moonquiet of two thousand stars
falling on Fourth Street in Panaca.
The smell of dust in October air.
A horse whinnies, dreams she is the wind.
On highway 319 a haytruck shifts toward Cedar City

and the night grows huge. I remember Basho,
  *Deep autumn,*
   *my neighbors,*
    *how do they live?—*

The high school basketball coach
dreaming a six foot five transfer student;
the county road supervisor, his stubbled face
creased by the white sheet;
the short-order cook at the Silver Cafe
asleep with the smell of onions on her hand.

# Unionville Spring

To change the water's flow, we went out at night
in her father's fields, moved tin aqueducts
from trench to trench. Cattle lowed in the pasture,
each of their solid shapes a darkness.
In rubber boots we slogged through muck knee-deep.
Trying to siphon a hose, I sucked too hard,
swallowed thick water & felt the silt
settle in my lungs. She heard me choke
& shined the light.
A large frog singled out in the beam,
leaped into dark. She laughed when she knew
I was all right. We fell into
the irrigation ditch, rolling, we welcomed each other
to good black mud.
                      What I hold to is night air
on my skin, stars
showing on the surface of the warm spring.
Our boots stand next to our clothes on the white rock
by the cutbank. When she dives into the pond
the splash of her body is an ovation.
I jump, scattering stars, to pull toward her.

# Rains

I watched Kate lift her skirt
to cross the irrigation ditch
that ran like a ragged shoelace
from the pond down through pasture.
There was disorder in the northern sky,
an approaching hem of jagged rain
& shaped clouds—one, an owl's mask,
another, a broken tea cup.

Above us, a ribbon of linnets hung in the air
gliding, gliding. I wanted a faith like that,
but on the path to the pond
we found one dead, fallen out of belief.

We picked blackberries on the way.
The berries sweet, the stings of blood
beading our wrists.
At the pond, we heard the evening song, blackbird
& rusty guttural of frog
mimicked by cattle in the field.
The air warm & musty like an old piano.

Two raindrops fell on the water & made a ring
like moonlight pinging off the hood of my father's truck
parked in front of the Double Hawk Tavern.
I wondered if those raindrops fell all that way
together, only to break apart near the end, or
if they fell separately & then joined the same water.

This was before I learned the language of men
& the crude ways they talk
of women & work & what they have lost.
The rain would come harder.
We would turn to go back.
She would lift her skirt to cross the ditch
& I would feel raindrops
falling on the linnet,
wings bent toward flight.

# Theory of Twilight

My brother's angular shadow is imitated
    by my father's dark outline
shimmering on the kitchen wall like water
    in the slanted light of a falling sun.
My father slices peaches and gives me

    a bowl of fleshy wedges
the color of a sky I saw in Molleñdo,
    a fishing town in Peru.
It was a sunset that remembered my brother.
    He thought the moment before death

must be like twilight, neither light or dark.
    In California the ocean
was five miles from my brother's hospital bed,
    lulling him to sleep
with a dream of waves he couldn't quite hear.

    I'd walk the shoreline
as he tossed, afternoons, drowsing.
    Kneeling, I freed the best shells
from black sand for him
    and, back again, told

about clocking the sun as it sank into the sea.
    For a week I'd timed it—
73 seconds from the moment
    the sun touched water
until it disappeared completely.

    My father rubs his knuckles
as if smoothing them. He knows more about guilt
    than I do. I am neither a husband
or a father. He is years sadder.
    While I was in Peru

looking out to sea, I saw my brother's paleness.
    He waited, palms-up, white
and bride-like. His eyes rolled toward the ceiling,
    his last breath left,
and a quiet assumed the room.

    Taped to the wall,
the card sent by Grandmother:
    a greeting card sunrise
or sunset. 73 seconds
    from the moment.

I took the card down and walked out
    into the hallway's sallow light. My parents
were coming toward me. Mother rushed the room,
    but we held her back. I'm not sure why.
She called out his name and her voice drifted

    back thirty years—a mother's evening song,
lilting across the deep-rutted road into the summer field,
    calling him home.
While my father entered the room, I held the pain—
    keeping grief

against her small shoulder until the door opened
    and he took her in.
A stunning sunset in Mollendo, and I
    was missing everyone I'd ever loved.
The door opened on the last glimpse of my brother.

    He was not as I had left him.
His father had touched his eyes closed, mothered
    the shock of black hair from his forehead
and made into prayer, finger by finger
    the hands.

# Three

# Yes

I believe in a map I followed
high into the Andes.
I say yes to the A encyclopedia,
yes to my mother who was too poor
to buy a set but collected free samples
of first volumes.
So I learned the presidents
whose names begin with "A"
and when my teachers asked for reports,
I said yes to the Adamses
and to Chester Alan Arthur
who came to office in 1881
when James Garfield was shot
by a disappointed office-seeker.
There are some things to which
I can't say no. I say yes, oh yes,
to your kisses,
yes to no, yes to rain,
its repetition. I say yes
to fallen leaves and the leaves
yet to let go. I say yes
to my student, Oudalay Phandonovoung, who told me
after a bird had crapped on my head,
that where he came from
I'd be considered a lucky man.

# Sophal Niem and the Moon in the Bucket

When the moon was highest,
her father would drop the family mirror
into a bucket of water, where
waves of light wobbled
until the mirror claimed the moon's full attention
& the reflection rippled white half a moment.
Then the moon knitted together & settled,
held still in the bucket.
When Sophal & her brother bowed close
to drink in the sight, they saw the bright moon
& within it the tree that Buddah sat under.

> Write about your most embarrassing moment—
> I give my Cambodian students
> the same assignment I have used
> for years in Nevada high schools.
> They ask,
> What does embarrassing mean?
> I tell them,
> It means a time when you were uncomfortable,
> a time when you felt everyone
> was watching you.

The moon above the prison camp
illuminated men & women,
cast their bound shadows
& revealed the path
when Sophal's family began walking
away from the fields,
past blindfolded skulls.
Later they watched the full moon in the river,
unable to cross, the bridge destroyed.
Her father let down his shoulder board
with the bucket swinging from one end.

At home I sit in a yellow circle of lamplight
reading my students' papers.
Sophal Niem tells about minefields
on the Cambodian-Thai border
& encountering robbers with rotten teeth.
They raped her in front of her family.
She watched her mother clench,
raise her eyes above what was happening.
Sophal writes, *I felt embarrassed.*
*It was uncomfortable.*

Sophal's father went down to the river
& returned with the bucket full.
He unwrapped a bundle & took out the mirror,
held it above the water & let it fall.
The moon, complete in the sky,
refused to hold the broken light
reflecting into splintered bone
on the water's smooth surface.

Her father reached for the mirror,
his hand dripping, & smashed it on a rock,
releasing the spirits of all the dead
who had ever looked into the glass.
Sophal found a piece,
held it & felt a keen edge.
She saw part of her face.
She told herself, *I am the mirror, I am not.*

# Salt

*for Shaun Griffin*

In the coastal Peruvian town of Molleñdo,
after the generator shuts down & the lights
are off in the sea shack
& the tide is right at night,
we shoulder our fishing net to the dark shoreline.
The sand, still warm with sun,
coats my feet like white ash.

Into the sea we wade together,
Manuel & Pedro in front of Lucho & me.
I joke in broken Spanish
about how often we seem to drag in nine fish—
nine shinings in the grid of rope—
three finger-sized anchovies, covina,
& sandy moons of flounder.

The water settles calm around our chests.
For a moment, the waves' repetition stops.
We stand still with the water, the wet rope
soaked & heavy on our shoulders.
I look out to where the drowned are cradled,
hold my breath & feel the ocean of my living blood.

Then the waves resume & we begin again.
The two in front spread the net in the water
while Lucho & I struggle for shore.
We pull the guide ropes in, gripping tight
to keep the rope from slipping.
My hand cramps. In the night I can't see,
not much. The shapes of men in near blue moonlight,
sparks where the sand kicks up.

We work the net many times
then build a fire with driftwood
& cook the anchovies crackling in a pan over flame.
We eat them hot & whole with warm beer,
the oil pearling on our lips, our fingers.

After carrying the catch back to the sea shack,
I lie down in my second summer of the year
& feel sand coarse against my scalp.
I can't read the constellations,
the moon is backwards in the sky.

At daybreak, the fishermen outside push their carts
stacked with fish. The wheels grinding to market.
I wake to sand on my lips,
brush the crusted salt from my arms.
When I stand & step away from the yellowed sheet
on the floor of splintered slats
that is my bed, I step from
a man's cast-off shape,
the shed salt, life made crystalline.

# Silver

*—Virginia City*

## 1.

1858
Goldminers curse the bluish mud
that clogs sluice boxes & rockers
used to collect placer gold. They muck
the blue stuff & toss it
beneath scrub pine in Six Mile Canyon
until they find the mud is silver rich.

## 2.

At night in the Crystal Bar
they pay 15¢ a long bit,
for double-bock beer
or lemonade with claret punch,
& dance quadrilles to 6/8 time.

## 3.

They speak a language:
    drifts & spurs
blackdamp upraise crosscut.

## 4.

An envelope of sun
pales the old photograph of miners,
shoulder to shoulder, stripped to the waist.
Their eyes the speckles
within white & blue-streaked quartz,
light inside rock.

# 5.

A snapped cable. The elevator car fell
three hundred feet, collapsed like cardboard.
Fourteen men lost deep in the Yellowjacket Mine.
Firemen flipped coins, fateful moons,
to see who would go down.
The wives stood in front of houses
on the hillside & realized
their worst, literal fear.
They knew before they were told
about fortune.

# Trajectory

You kneel
and take the arrowhead
from where it lies, from where
it has been waiting,
and lift it

into the present
unresolved in arcing
shafts of light. The obsidian
is the blue-black
of crow feathers.

You scrape the stone
with a fingernail, work loose
the rouge of old dust.
And the tip you thought dulled
cuts.

# Test

> *"You people who live near Nevada Test Site are in a very real sense active participants in the Nation's atomic test program."*
>
> —Atomic Energy Booklet, page 2, March, 1957

The sky brightens with a flash.

A rancher feels the earth shudder
beneath his red roan.
He shields his eyes—
flesh is transparent,
his hand a diagram of bones.
*My God*, he whispers.

The mare shies,
only the pressure of his boots
urges her
through Eagle Valley to a ridge where
the only boundary
is the sky.

In the sparse shade of a Joshua tree
the pink clouds hover
over the ranges of his retina.

He rubs his burning nostrils
& tries to spit out the bitterness,

the metallic taste.

# Boundaries

Last night they watched a fish leap
completely out of the water.
For a moment
it was suspended
above its mirrored image,
until it fell
breaking the surface.

This morning the light is the softness
of a sharp fingernail run down the spine.
Beyond the motel window, the light
remakes the trees that edge the lake.
There are wakes on the water,
Tahoe's cold glinting.

Asleep in the posture of dream,
their bodies are boundaries.
His breath warm on her neck, a shadow
bends to the curve of her breast.
The border of their bodies
shape to one another.

Years ago, the first night,
a new bath towel & the colors ran,
tinged their bodies blue
so that their flesh flared,
a mackereled sunrise sky.

They have come to the stateline resort
to try to reclaim something
of that bluing flesh.

After showering he finds her
nude, on the floor
sketching herself in the full-mirrored
closet door. "It's very pretty,"
he says to her reflection.
She frowns, "I try to see past
the flaws, but it's difficult."

He reaches for her. She takes his hand
& she rises to stand beside him.
She tosses her pencilled self on the bed.

They hold each other, press together
tight in the simple desire to fit.
In the mirror there are still spaces between them,
places where they don't touch,
that they might rise above
a moment before they descend
& fall blue through themselves.

# On a Windy Afternoon

I stop for gas in Carlin.
In the schoolyard students
exercise in rows. Arms & legs
scissoring into an X
then closing to an I.

For someone it is laundry day.
The breeze slips inside
clothes on the line
inspiring bodies of wind.
Shirts wave to passersby,
& crazy-legged pants try to run
          away.

In this town
there's probably a meal cooking,
a woman I could love, a bed
I would find comfortable.

When the tank is filled,
I drive for Battle Mountain.

# The Waiting

## 1.

The taillights far ahead recall the glow
of cigarettes my father smoked in the dark
those nights I stayed out late.
I had a curfew of conscience; knew
he couldn't sleep till I was home.
It was late. I'd been drinking cheap red wine
and when I reached the front door,
I still held the rainbow barrette
I'd taken from Charlene Moore's hair.
My father's silhouette waited in the darkest corner.
I ignored him. And he said nothing.
The bedroom door creaked as I closed it.
Minutes later, the door creaked again,
a fan of light opening across the floor.
He leaned over me,
pulling blankets up under my chin.
There was a hush
as in the backseat of a car
when a girl's bra unhooks.
His breath tobacco-sweet, the stubble
of his whiskers prickling
as he kissed my cheek.

## 2.

My brother looked tiny in the hospital bed.
Each day I took his hands they were colder.
Thirteen years apart—when I was younger
he seemed more father than brother.
Now his face had thinned back
to a sharply-chiseled teenager's,
and the nurses thought I looked older than he did.
We finally talked about growing up,
the difference between the '50's and '60's.
I told him about the night Dad tucked me in,
kissed me goodnight. He wasn't surprised.
Shortly before going away to college
he and Jimmy Nielson drove to San Francisco
in Nielson's red '56 T-Bird,
returning home late and drunk.
He slipped quickly to his room.
Soon he realized Dad was standing by the bed.
We laughed, thinking of our father as a specter
who arrived on nights we drank too much.

# 3.

In my parents' house history is lost.
In other homes after someone has passed on
into darkness, there are little shrines—
photographs of the dead on top of the television
or on the shelf beside glass swans.
Graduation pictures of my brother and me
have been taken from the wall.
It was a long time
before my father looked directly at anyone.
He won't talk about it.
This morning I watched him
put on his coat of silence
and walk out to the woodpile,
snow blossoming in his greying hair.
He splits wood to exhaust himself;
in this way my father teaches me
the sorrow of pine, cedar, and oak.
There is enough wood for three winters.
Tonight we watch the 10:00 news on channel 2.
My mother goes to bed; we watch the 11:00 news
    on channel 3.
I say goodnight and go to my old room—
the familiar quilt and reading lamp.
In the hospital, my brother was so still
I moved close to find a breath there.
I kissed his pale cheek, touched
my warm lips to his skin.
Now my father sits alone by the fire,
embers burning to white ash.
If he looks out the window, he will see
his own face looking in.
He has lost his son in the night
and he is waiting for him.

*Gary Short lives in the shadow of an abandoned mill at American Flat, a few miles down a dirt road from Virginia City, Nevada. After graduating from California State University, Fresno, he studied at California State University, Sacramento, and Arizona State University. He worked as a high school teacher and as an artist-in-residence in Nevada schools. Short has been poetry editor for* **Hayden's Ferry Review** *and* **Shankpainter**. *A 1990-91 Writing Fellow at the Fine Arts Work Center in Provincetown, he is a 1993-95 Wallace Stegner Fellow at Stanford.*

# Ahsahta Press
## MODERN & CONTEMPORARY POETRY OF THE AMERICAN WEST

Sandra Alcosser, *A Fish To Feed All Hunger*
David Axelrod, *Jerusalem of Grass*
*David Baker, *Laws of the Land*
*Conger Beasley, Jr., *Over DeSoto's Bones*
Linda Bierds, *Flights of the Harvest Mare*
Richard Blessing, *Winter Constellations*
*Peggy Pond Church, *New & Selected Poems*
Katharine Coles, *The One Right Touch*
Wyn Cooper, *The Country of Here Below*
*Judson Crews, *The Clock of Moss*
H.L. Davis, *Selected Poems*
*Susan Strayer Deal, *The Dark Is a Door
            No Moving Parts*
*Gretel Ehrlich, *To Touch the Water*
Julie Fay, *Portraits of Women*
*Thomas Hornsby Ferril, *Anvil of Roses
            Westering*
*Hildegarde Flanner, *The Hearkening Eye*
Charley John Greasybear, *Songs*
Corrinne Hales, *Underground*
Hazel Hall, *Selected Poems*
Nan Hannon, *Sky River*
Gwendolen Haste, *Selected Poems*
Sonya Hess, *Kingdom of Lost Waters*
Cynthia Hogue, *The Woman in Red*
*Robert Krieger, *Headlands, Rising*
Elio Emiliano Ligi, *Disturbances*
Haniel Long, *My Seasons*
*Norman Macleod, *Selected Poems*
Ken McCullough, *Sycamore•Oriole*
Barbara Meyn, *The Abalone Heart*
Dixie Partridge, *Deer in the Haystacks*
Gerrye Payne, *The Year-God*
George Perreault, *Curved Like An Eye*

Howard W. Robertson, *to the fierce guard in the Assyrian Saloon*
*Leo Romero, *Agua Negra*
          *Going Home Away Indian*
Philip St. Clair, *At the Tent of Heaven*
          *Little-Dog-Of-Iron*
Donald Schenker, *Up Here*
Gary Short, *Theory of Twilight*
*Richard Speakes, *Hannah's Travel*
Genevieve Taggard, *To the Natural World*
*Marnie Walsh, *A Taste of the Knife*
Bill Witherup, *Men at Work*
*Carolyne Wright, *Stealing the Children*

*Women Poets of the West:An Anthology, 1850-1950*

*Selections from these volumes, read by their authors, are available on *The Ahsahta Cassette Sampler.*